2000 MEGA Things to spot

igloobooks

Can you find 1001 Dinosaur things?

ROAR! Welcome to a dinosaur adventure! There's all sorts of things going on in Dinoland, from Roger Raptor's birthday bash to the Meteor Music Festival. Each picture in this book has lots of different and interesting things for you to search and find. In fact, there are over 1000 things to find in Dinoland! Terry T-Rex and Stegosaurus Stan are in each picture, so you need to find them first. Then each page has little pictures to show you what else you need to search for, from Pre-historic Pop to Sabre Tooth Tigers!

Terry T-Rex   **Stegosaurus Stan**

Let's have a practice. Can you spot Terry T-Rex and Stegosaurus Stan? Once you've found them, see if you can spot these items as well in the picture on the opposite page.

1 Aeroplane   **5 Squirrels**   **10 Frogs**

Carnivore Cafe

It's the weekend and that's when Carnivore Café is at its busiest! See if you can find Terry T-Rex and Stegosaurus Stan amongst all the other customers.

Specials:
Pre-historic Pie
Dino Dumplings
Swampy Soup

See if you can spot these things at Carnivore Café, too.

1 Menu Board Pen

2 Aprons

3 Chef Hats

4 Plants

5 Steaks

6 Mugs of Hot Chocolate

7 Menus

8 Salt Shakers

9 Bottles of Ketchup

10 Snails

20 Forks

Fossil Beach

It's a sunny day on Fossil Beach and all of the dinosaurs are having fun in the sun.
Once you've found Stegosaurus Stan and Terry T-Rex, try spotting all of the other things, too!

4 Rainbow Fish

5 Lizards

6 Rubber Rings

7 Crabs

Can you find all of these other items on the beach, too?

1 Footprint

2 Pterodactyls

3 Bone-shaped Surfboards

8 Sun Hats

9 Umbrellas

10 Ice Creams

20 Sea Shells

Prehistoric Party

It's Roger Raptor's birthday. He's having a big party and everyone's invited. Can you spot Terry T-Rex and Stegosaurus Stan amongst the guests?

See if you can spot these things at the party, too.

1 Caveman Clown

2 Bubble Machines

3 Party Horns

4 Chocolate Bars

5 Red Balloons

6 Party Hats

7 Prehistoric Pop

8 Green Presents

9 Birthday Cards

10 Party Bags

20 Blue Bows

It's the annual music festival and this year
The Bone Bashers are playing a gig.
Can you see if Terry T-Rex and Stegosaurus
Stan are amongst the crowd?

Can you find these things at the festival, too?

 **1 Drum Kit**

 **2 Tents**

 **3 Microphones**

 **4 Blankets**

 **5 Speakers**

 **6 Cell Phones**

 **7 Glow Worms**

 **8 Band T-Shirts**

 **9 Money Pouches**

10 Welly Boots

 **20 Love Hearts**

The Reptile Races

Every year the dinosaurs and cavemen have a sports day. This year there are even more events! Can you spot Terry T-Rex and Stegosaurus Stan?

4 Shot Puts

5 Stop Watches

6 Javelins

7 Blue Shorts

When you've found Terry and Stan, see if you can find these things as well.

1 Bike

2 Trampolines

3 Whistles

8 Worms

9 Kit Bags

10 Bottles of Pop

20 Orange Segments

Fossil Fair

Everyone's been excited about the fair coming to town and now it's here! Can you spot where Terry T-Rex and Stegosaurus Stan are?

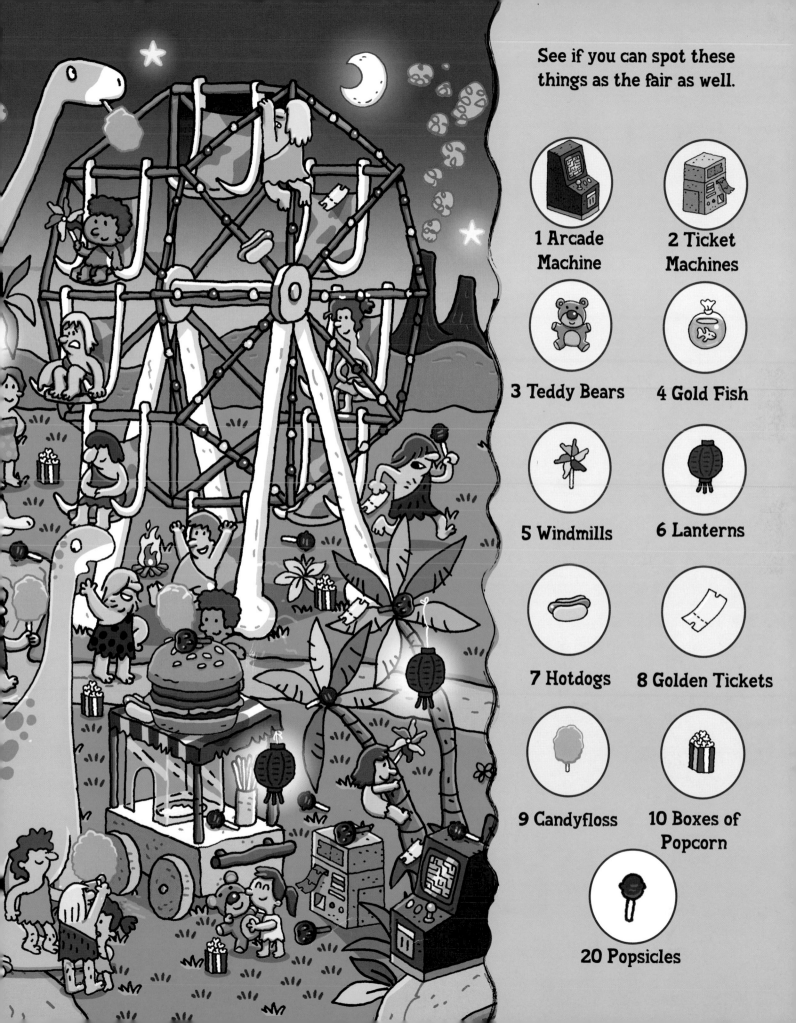

See if you can spot these things as the fair as well.

1 Arcade Machine

2 Ticket Machines

3 Teddy Bears

4 Gold Fish

5 Windmills

6 Lanterns

7 Hotdogs

8 Golden Tickets

9 Candyfloss

10 Boxes of Popcorn

20 Popsicles

Jurassic Jumble

Lots of dinosaurs love shopping at the local market.
See if you can spot Terry T-Rex and Stegosaurus Stan
in the crowd?

4 Footballs

5 Cricket Bats

6 Banana Signs

7 Yellow Books

Now you've found Terry and Stan, see if you can spot these things.

1 Chalk Board

2 Tennis Rackets

3 Pineapples

8 Balls of Wool

9 Prawns

10 Jars of Marbles

20 Tennis Balls

Herbivore Hill

It's been snowing and all of the dinosaurs and cavemen are ready with their skis and sledges at Herbivore Hill. Can you see what Terry T-Rex and Stegosaurus Stan are doing in the snow?

See if you can spot these on Herbivore Hill, too.

1 Yeti

2 Snowboarding Mice

3 Green Snowboards

4 Tobogans

5 Red Goggles

6 Blue Hats

7 Stripy Scarves

8 Yellow Gloves

9 Flags

10 Big Snowballs

20 Snowflakes

Asteroid Academy

Everyone has so much fun at Asteroid Academy!
Can you spot where Terry T-Rex and Stegosaurus
Stan are?

4 Pencil Holders

5 Pieces of Chalk

6 Calculators

7 Rulers

Can you find these things in the classroom, as well?

1 Clock

2 Globes

3 Blue Satchels

Pairs of scissors

9 Paper planes

10 Pens

20 Apples

Triassic Rock

The dinosaurs are having fun painting at Triassic Rock, even if it is a little messy! Can you find Terry T-Rex and Stegosaurus Stan amongst the painters?

Once you've spotted Terry and Stan, try finding these things, too.

1 Statue

2 Sloths

3 Bowls of fruit

4 Easels

5 Paint Rollers

6 Pallettes

7 Aprons

8 Water Pots

9 Brushes

10 Paint Prints

20 Paint Tubes

Well done! You found everything in Dinoland! Now go back and see if you can find each of these extra items in every picture, too.

 1 Nest

 1 Triceratops

 1 Baby Dinosaur

 1 Club

 1 Car

 1 Fire

 1 Spider

 1 Caveman with Polkadot Tunic

 1 Saber Tooth Tiger

 1 Woolly Mammoth

 1 Cave Painting

Wow! You found them all! How closely were you looking though? Do you know which picture each of these items is in?

 10 Beach Bags

 10 Cupcakes

 10 Toffee Apples

 10 Burgers

 10 Mosquitoes

 10 Note pads

 10 Ladybugs

 10 Candles

 10 Penguins

 10 Trolleys

Can you find...
1001 Pirate Things?

Can you find 1001 Pirate Things?

Ahoy me hearties! Welcome to a pirate adventure! There's all sorts of things going on at Pirate Island, from big parties to exciting treasure hunts. Each picture in this book has lots of different and interesting things for you to search and find. In fact, there are over 1000 things to find on Pirate Island! Swashbuckling Sid and One-eyed Eddie are in each picture, so you need to find them first. Then each page has little pictures to show you what else you need to search for, from gold doubloons to scurrying rats!

Swashbuckling Sid   One-eyed Eddie

Let's have a practice. Can you spot Swashbuckling Sid and One-eyed Eddie in the picture on the opposite page. Once you've found them, see if you can spot these items as well:

2 Canons   5 Eye Patches   10 Mice

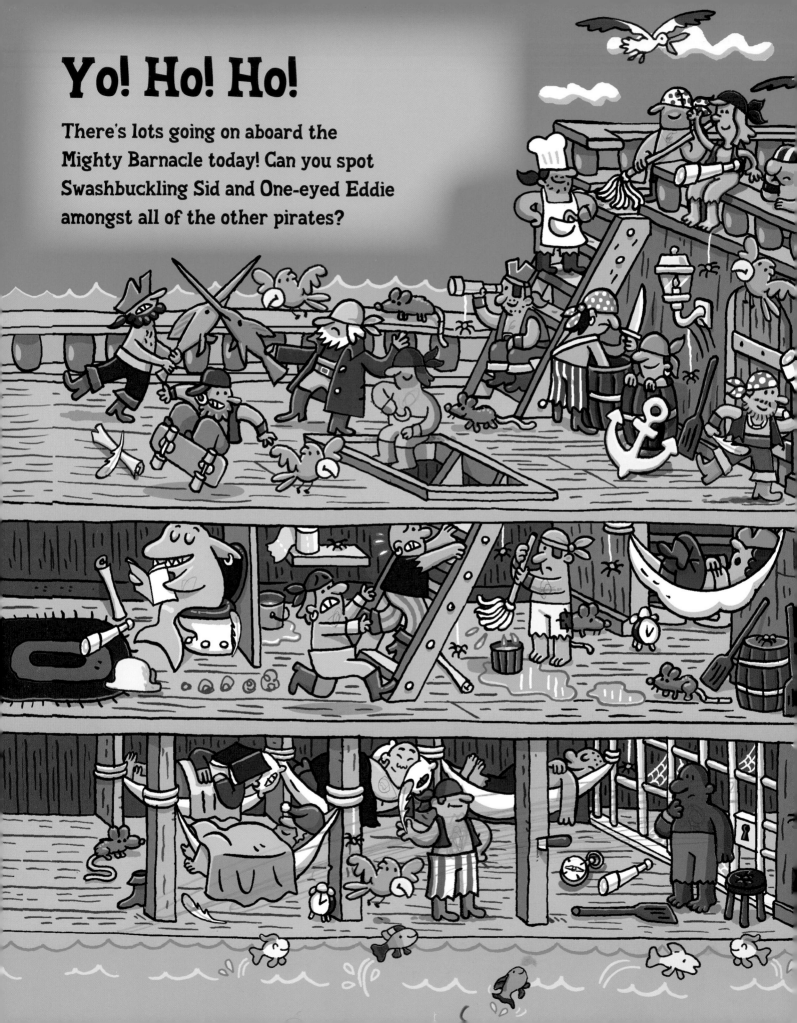

Yo! Ho! Ho!

There's lots going on aboard the
Mighty Barnacle today! Can you spot
Swashbuckling Sid and One-eyed Eddie
amongst all of the other pirates?

Once you've found Sid and Eddie, see if you can find these things, too.

1 Skateboard

2 Clocks

3 Mops

4 Oars

5 Barrels

6 Hammocks

7 Pieces of Parchment

8 Parrots

9 Telescopes

10 Gold Earrings

20 Spiders

Davey Jones' Locker

In the depths of the deep, blue sea, the pirates have found an ancient shipwreck! Can you spot Swashbuckling Sid and One-eyed Eddie swimming around?

Can you find these things in and around the shipwreck, too?

1 Diving Suit

2 Seals

3 Lobsters

4 Angler Fish

5 Sea Urchins

6 Jelly Fish

7 Seahorses

8 Red & Yellow Fish

9 Pink Coral

10 Anemones

20 Bubbles

Get Yer Pirate Booty Here!

The pirates have found a map and they're off to find some treasure! Can you find Swashbuckling Sid and One-eyed Eddie on the map?

4 Water Pouches

5 Shovels

6 Knotted Ropes

7 Padlocks

See if you can find these things on the treasure map, too.

1 Treasure Chest

2 Camels

3 Vultures

8 Bones

9 Shark Fins

10 Footprints

20 Flies

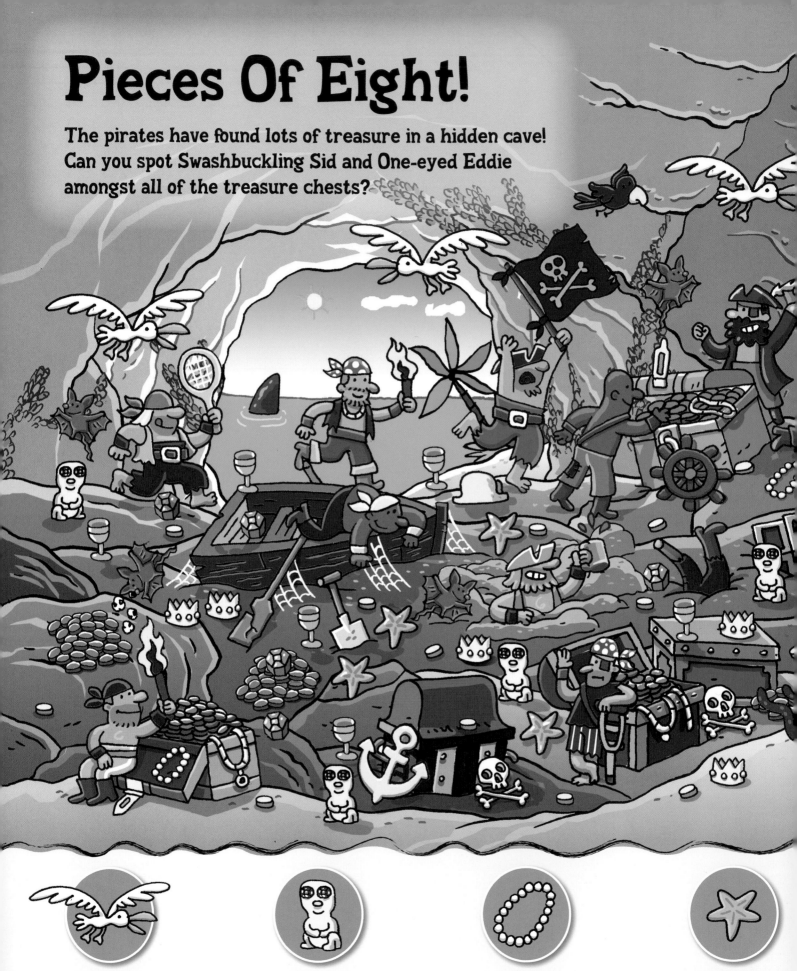

Pieces Of Eight!

The pirates have found lots of treasure in a hidden cave! Can you spot Swashbuckling Sid and One-eyed Eddie amongst all of the treasure chests?

4 Seagulls

5 Gold Statues

6 Pearl Necklaces

7 Starfish

Can spot these things hidden in the cave, as well.

1 Boat

2 Torches

3 Skull and Crossbones

8 Crowns

9 Silver Goblets

10 Bats

20 Gold Doubloons

Shiver Me Timbers!

The pirates are making their way through the jungle, back to their ship with their treasure loot! See if you can find Swashbuckling Sid and One-eyed Eddie.

Can you spot these items in the jungle, too?

1 Volcano

2 Crocodiles

3 Bears

4 Tigers

5 Toucans

6 Pocket Watches

7 Snakes

8 Stars

9 Bags of Treasure

10 Tropical Flowers

20 Purple Leaves

Land Ahoy!

The pirates are visiting a nearby town to stock up on food. Can you spot Swashbuckling Sid and One-eyed Eddie? What's Swashbuckling Sid carrying?

If you've found Sid and Eddie,
try spotting these things, too.

1 Wanted
Poster

2 Horses

3 Money
Pouches

4 Stone
Gargoyles

5 Lamps

6 Wooden
Boxes

7 Apples

8 Cutlasses

9 Green
Bottles

10 Cannonballs

20 Rats

A Buccaneer Banquet!

The pirates are having a banquet to celebrate finding lots of treasure! Can you spot Swashbuckling Sid and One-eyed Eddie amongst all the fun at the feast?

4 Red Spotty Bandanas

5 Mouldy Blocks of Cheese

6 Party Poppers

7 Fish Bones

When you've spotted Sid and Eddie, hunt for these items, too.

1 Accordian

2 Cakes

3 Loaves of Bread

8 Blue Balloons

9 Party Hats

10 Chicken Drumsticks

20 Boiled Sweets

Kitchen Chaos!

The pirates are busy preparing for a huge feast.
Can you find Swashbuckling Sid and One-eyed
Eddie amongst the chaos?

Search for these items in the
pirate kitchen, as well.

1 Menu

2 Stoves

3 Brooms

4 Flour Bags

5 Mugs

6 Stew Pots

7 Forks

8 Carrots

9 Whisks

10 Potatos

20 Beetles

Beach Fun

The pirates are relaxing at the beach today. See if you can spot Swashbuckling Sid and One-eyed Eddie having fun in the sun.

4 Picnic Hampers

5 Red buckets

6 Ice-creams

7 Yellow Towels

See if you can find these items at the beach, too.

1 Umbrella

2 Fruity drinks

3 Sandcastles

8 Coconuts

9 Bottles of Sun cream

10 Crabs

20 Shells

Sea Sports

It's sports day and the pirates are having a race! Can you spot Swashbuckling Sid and One-eyed Eddie?

4 Turtles

5 Butterflies

6 Bottles of Water

7 Life Rings

Can you spot these extra pirate items, too?

1 Trophy

2 Megaphones

3 Lilos

8 Goggles

9 Cameras

10 Medals

20 Bees

Avast ye matey! You found everything on Pirate Island! Now go back and see if you can find each of these extra items in every picture, too.

1 Yellow Pirate Hat

1 Octopus

1 Monkey

1 Pirate Chef

1 Skeleton

1 Treasure Map

1 Wheel

1 Captain

1 Jolly Roger Flag

1 Anchor

1 Compass

How closely were you looking? Do you know which picture each of these items were in?

10 palm trees

10 emeralds

10 red flags

10 feathers

10 chickens

10 beach balls

10 limpets

10 candles

10 spoons

10 dragonflies